Triangles of Light

THE EDWARD HOPPER POEMS

Other works by James Hoggard:

FICTION

Trotter Ross
Elevator Man
Riding the Wind and Other Tales
Patterns of Illusion

POETRY

Eyesigns
The Shaper Poems
Two Gulls, One Hawk
Breaking an Indelicate Statue
Medea in Taos
Rain in a Sunlit Sky
Wearing the River

TRANSLATION

The Art of Dying, poems by Oscar Hahn
Love Breaks, poems by Oscar Hahn
Chronicle of My Worst Years, poems by Tino Villanueva
Alone Against the Sea: Poems from Cuba, by Raúl Mesa
Splintered Silences, poems by Greta de León
Stolen Verses & Other Poems, by Oscar Hahn
Ashes In Love, poems by Oscar Hahn

*Triangles
of Light*

THE EDWARD HOPPER POEMS

BY

JAMES HOGGARD

WingsPress

SAN ANTONIO, TEXAS
2009

Triangles of Light © 2009 by James Hoggard
Cover art: "Sun in An Empty Room," 1963, by Edward Hopper,
used by permission of the Whitney Museum of American Art.
Page 2: "Approaching a City," 1946, by Edward Hopper,
used by permission of the Phillips Collection, Washington, D.C.
Page 28: "Night on the El Train," 1920, by Edward Hopper,
used by permission of the British Museum of Art, London.
Page 52: "Italian Quarter, Gloucester," 1912, by Edward Hopper,
used by permission of the Whitney Museum of American Art, New York.

First Edition

ISBN-13: 978-0-916727-55-0

Wings Press
627 E. Guenther
San Antonio, Texas 78210
Phone/fax: (210) 271-7805

On-line catalogue and ordering:
www.wingspress.com
All Wings Press titles are distributed to the trade by
Independent Publishers Group
www.ipgbook.com

Library of Congress Cataloging-in-Publication Data:

Hoggard, James.
  Triangles of light : the Edward Hopper poems / by James Hoggard. -- 1st ed.
    p. cm.
  Includes index.
  ISBN 978-0-916727-55-0 (pbk. : alk. paper)
  1. Hopper, Edward, 1882-1967--Poetry. I. Title.
  PS3558.O34752T75 2009
  811'.54--dc22
                            2009004223

CONTENTS

III

"I saw Paradise in the dust of the street."

— Denise Levertov, from "City Psalm"

"But it was Hopper ... who saw that the old frontier had moved inward and now lay within the self."

— Robert Hughes, *American Visions: The Epic History of Art in America*

ACKNOWLEDGMENTS

Acknowledgment is made to the following publications where most of these poems first appeared: *Borderlands, Cape Rock, Clackamas Literary Review, The Crab Creek Review, Descant, The Dirty Goat, Faultline, Image: A Journal of the Arts and Religion, Janus Head, Langdon Review, Manoa, The Prague Review,* and *Windhover.* Special thanks also to Anita Duquette, Whitney Museum of American Art, for her expertise.

PREFACE

One of the most narratively suggestive image-makers in modern American realism, Edward Hopper often structured his work geometrically; yet his paintings and etchings evoke voices. This curious blend of characteristics informing his work suggests a layering of effects rather than fragmentation. That fact in itself suggests why his work is so narratively rich, why his imagery gives us a continually interesting articulation of the tension between will and restraint that names the modern American voice, especially the male's. One thinks, of course, of the word laconic, what often seems to be a stinginess of language that's a cousin of anger. At the same time, silences in Hopper often seem still, sometimes oddly lyrical, even when his imagery depicts the inelegance of streets and scenes behind windows.

Studying his images, we find ourselves looking at characters – even inanimate things – that provoke speech. Points of intimacy, however, are rarely reached, and when they are, as in "Les Deux Pigeons" or "Night On The El Train," one notices a tone of bemusement that counters the pleasure of erotic nostalgia. Although there may be threats of explosion imminent in his portrayal of couples and individuals who seem unable or disinclined to communicate intimately with each other – as we see in the ambiguities in "Cape Cod Evening" and "Four Lane Road" – one realizes that something different from anxiety is being depicted in Hopper's work. His empty streets and sometimes peopleless rooms do not seem lonely; rather, they seem uncluttered, happily devoid of foolishly chatty people; and some of his figures, whether alone or in the presence of an "other," seem strangely serene in their non-involvement, as if momentary non-attachment is, if not altogether welcome, certainly tolerable. That fact, too, is curious. Perhaps the subjects' lack of strong expression leaves them looking sufficiently blank to draw our attention toward them, to provide them with a fuller sense of personality than their surfaces articulate directly. Things like that often occur when one is in the presence of understatement. One thinks of the style and effects of stories by Hopper's contemporaries Sherwood Anderson and Ernest Hemingway. One also thinks of the ironically stirring blankness of presence shared by many of the culture's great beauties from the first half-century of the movies. Because those women often gave us little by way of precise expression, we rushed our attention toward them. We had to. The blankness of their look was so provocative it proved magnetic. That blankness made us anxious, and anxiety suggested a weakness we wanted to overcome. The storytellers, though, were ahead of us.

Thinking about the tenor of the world described by the interpreters of modernism, one recalls how often terms like alienation, anxiety, and fragmentation have been used. All of those conditions suggest weakness. The major American modernists, however, whether literary or pictorial, commonly brought energy and toughness to their art. That's one of the reasons why they became important, influential to Europeans and South Americans alike. Even in T.S. Eliot's landmark work of modernism, "The Waste Land," one finds that, although characters in the drama might be weak, even at times pitiful, a powerful sense of vitality guides the poem toward its symphonically dramatic ending. One finds similar energy and certainty of purpose in other American voices like Kate Chopin, Eugene O'Neill, William Faulkner, Ernest Hemingway, William Carlos Williams, Eudora Welty and others in literature, and in painters like Winslow Homer, John Singer Sargent, James A. M.

Whistler, George Bellows, Thomas Hart Benton, John Steuart Curry, and Andrew Wyeth. Edward Hopper is as vibrantly narrative and as darkly lyrical as any of them.

Hopper's work caught my attention early. I was ten years old and in an art class that Mrs. Ruth Dickson taught at Crockett Elementary School. Besides helping us develop our varying abilities with penmanship, watercolor, tempera, India ink, and the new oil crayons called Sketcho sticks that allowed one to create all kinds of textures and blends with the imaginative use of an eraser, she taught us art history. She regularly showed us slides of the work of the European masters, and just as often she showed us slides of major American figures, including a lot of painters who were still working, some of them not much past mid-career. I loved the class and mistakenly assumed that all fifth, sixth, and seventh graders had similar art classes. I later discovered they didn't. I had just gotten lucky. For three years, September into May, I was offered a wealth of important information about aesthetics in the culture I was a part of. For years I also idly remembered that the best work I did during that time was a lighthouse that I used Sketcho crayons to present. I even forgot, until I was well into writing the poems included in *Triangles of Light,* that the piece had been a copy of a painting by Hopper. Something about the man – the work he did – intrigued me, and it wasn't primarily his draftsmanship. Others were just as good, and many better.

One night, years before I began these poems, I found myself sketching out a poem that I would title "Motel." The poem depicted a solitary woman who was trying to be stony about her own grief, but however hard she tried she couldn't lose herself altogether: the plainness of her room and the fact of her flesh stayed vivid enough to keep her from disappearing into unconsciousness. The fact of the world was insistently present, and well before the poem was finished I was thinking of it as a copy of one of Hopper's paintings – but I had never seen this image in his work. The mood of the piece, however, seemed to be his; so giving in to whimsy, I subtitled the poem: "Based On A Painting That Edward Hopper Never Did."

Years later I was in Denver to see my son who was working then in Meininger's Art Supply Store. After showing me numerous fountain pens – he and I are both partial to them – he guided me to where the art books were. I was going to browse through them while he took care of tasks. I came upon Lloyd Goodrich's 1993 edition of *Edward Hopper*. Thumbing through it, I was startled when I came upon a reproduction of a painting whose image was eerily close to the one in my poem. The power of the recognition thrilled me. At the same moment a sales woman, one of my son's colleagues, came up and asked if I were finding everything I wanted. The large book still open in my hands, I told her I had just discovered a painting that a poem of mine had depicted, though I had never seen a copy of the painting till now. Then I found another painting whose image and mood were parallel to those in the poem. I had to have the book. Operating on impulse, I said I was going to do a series of poems on Hopper's paintings. The more pages I turned the more excited I got, but I had no idea that I'd do more than several poems on the subject. A couple months after that I started looking carefully at Hopper's famous "Nighthawks," three customers and short-order cook in an urban diner late at night. I noticed how many triangles there were in the piece. In fact, everything in the painting seemed to be associated with triangles. The same geometry, I came to see, was prominent in other works as well. The shape, in fact, appeared dominant; I began to wonder what that meant.

I started working on a poem based on "Nighthawks." Experimenting – let's call it playing – I tried the narration from several points of view. Before long I tried still another one, then soon was studying another painting. I knew now what the voice saying these pieces needed to be: Hopper's, not mine or a series of voices, but Hopper's own contrarian voice. He had good demons to fight, and I let the paintings keep working on me. I thought about the dramas implied by them. I thought about the way they were structured. More systematically than before I studied Hopper himself. My instincts about him had been accurate. Exploring Gail Levin's richly textured *Edward Hopper: An Intimate Biography* (Knopf, 1995) and other works to check and doublecheck my perceptions with specific information, I wrote poem after poem. I knew my scheme now: Hopper was telling the poems, and standing in for an audience, I followed his observations. He had important things to say, and a good amount of it was unapologetically rough.

A lot of American male artists in his time and later had not felt comfortable talking about aesthetics or discussing their own work. Faulkner, for heavensakes, had even tried passing himself off as a farmer. Those figures, however, had assimilated and developed a wealth of information, and one of them was going to start talking. Each of the poems would have Hopper responding to a particular painting or etching whose title would name the poem. Day after day and month after month I wrote and rewrote the works until I'd done fifty of them. It was time to structure the collection. A number of the poems were already coming out in publications. I felt I was on to something big, not just about Hopper but about the artist in America.

Hopper's sensibility, gritty and sometimes ungiving as it was, seemed to name, in effect, a major portion of a nation, the artist in response to ideas and environment, and the thorny relationship between men and women. In contrast to the European model, the American artist had often seemed curiously inarticulate with the softer emotions but blazingly forthright in expressing the negative ones. Talk about love and aesthetics was rare; and often, when it occurred, the conversation seemed strained. Anger, however, came easily. The profane seemed more at hand than the sacred. Ironically, Puritanism worked into the model, but so did other edges and layers of America. One thought of Henry Adams's "The Dynamo And The Virgin," and Adams's comment that in America sex as force had found little expression except in Walt Whitman. The Virgin Mary was Western civilization's incarnation of the goddess, the female power of generation in a cosmos whose traditional descriptions had intimated anthropomorphic elements; but in America the figure had seemed either taboo or simply absent as a major point of reference: beside the point to gadgetry and machinery. Sex in America had meant sin much more than it had seemed an embodiment of the cosmically generative force that we were all a part of whether we embraced it or not. In fact, except in gestures of rebellion or in minor pockets of North America, the Virgin had not seemed a major or even worthy point of reference at all. An emblem of science and technology, the dynamo, the electric generator – so comfortably non-protoplasmic yet so insentient and indifferent to its users – was becoming both god and altar. Thinking about such matters, I began seeing the purpose, the appropriateness of Hopper's triangles. A non-human – even non-living – presence seemed necessary to give his work dependable meaning and shape. Geometry was both crutch and guide. So what if the world of modernism had become dissembled, shaky with undependability, abysmally antiheroic and fragmentary as well as troublesomely (or promisingly) democratic? No shape was more stable than the triangle. Nothing matched it for preventing collapse.

I kept rewriting the works. Cragginess, after all, demanded its own kind of polish, and I realized that I had been preparing to do this work for decades. The major points of concern, however, went far beyond the personal, even when they embraced the personal, or suddenly seemed baldly paradoxical, as they did when, to be authentic, one had to be inelegantly elegant. Mark Twain had intuited and demonstrated just that, and so had other major American figures near his time and after it. In spite of some important gestures toward the sacred, modern American literature seemed predominately secular. One thought of Robert Frost. One thought of William Carlos Williams, a man and artist Hopper admired. One even thought of Emily Dickinson and the peculiar yet effective hitches in her rhythms. Those rhythmic hitches are reflective of what she called the "lunacy of light." One thought of so many. One thought of the culture one had been born into, a culture that longed for tradition while defying it. Suddenly the obvious emerged. Hopper's triangles weren't decorative but necessary to give at least an illusory, coherent shape to an intense but godless and pointless world. Art was the way toward meaning. To be authentic, though, the work had to acknowledge the non-order it sprang from.

A comment by Hopper's talented wife and perpetual model Jo kept coming to mind. She said that having a conversation with him was like dropping a stone down a well – except when the stone hits bottom, you hear it, "but with Eddie you don't get anything back" – except art, and a story-centered one at that. Hopper's implied narratives look simultaneously simple and complex, and so they should, for they imply multilevel conversations with self and the world and those extensions of self, the things one makes that tradition calls art.

– James Hoggard

I.

"Approaching a City" (1946)

The Phillips Collection, Washington, D.C.

APPROACHING A CITY

(EH on his 1946 oil)

Whether you have in mind talk
or other intrusive atmosphere
I'll remind you: movement and sound
often bother me – chatter's offensive
and I don't like the habit many have
of interrupting good spreads of light
If they'd ditch their shadow before me,
but not their mass, I'd be pleased

I know that you and others too
have said the world that I depict
seems God-abandoned, and that all
my lightless portals – empty doorways
and rows of glassless windows –
hum with a damn nostalgia for death,
but that's wrong, most often wrong –
I simply have moods,
and I'm moving toward one now

Everything turns, in time, toward myth –
What? Sure, I'll talk you through this piece,
and I'll talk you through some others, too
You caught me right –
the tunnel's darkness soothes me
and I prefer my windows without glass
There are 58 of them here, and not
a one's involved with grief or God

It was Sunday, simply Sunday morning
and I, in the memory I've depicted,
was coming back home on the train
I'd been awake all night,
and glad the goddamn trip was done,
I liked the fact no nuisances were out:
neither racket nor motion nor people:
just a tunnel, my entrance home,
a tunnel to lead me smoothly home

NIGHT IN THE PARK

(EH on his 1921 etching)

Of course, I placed him there,
the man at the end of a bench,
his back's forward roll curving him
into the paper he's reading
in a pool of spilling light,
the bulb barely in view above him,

and the blur of foliage
fanned around him
is at least as visible as he is,
and as important as he is,
shadow and light being life to me

And as he reads I notice that
his knees and feet triangulate
the pond of light he's sitting in:
the shape of light conveyed
in much the way that darkness is,
as passive space,
the void between the stars:
a terror to some,
but pleasure to me

MOONLIGHT INTERIOR

(EH on his 1921–23 oil)

I only remember moments now,
my brush the mnemonic device
through which I discover
and sometimes even invent
events of a fragmentary past

The brevity of it still an ache,
she seems like a glance in a dream
whose textures are blurred,
but her auburn hair is loose,
like the moon-white curtain's gasp,

and the gable across the way
is an eye in tension with mine,
but I no longer see
the woman's face –
she's stepping away from me,

but as she does I see
the moon's soft light
sliding down the length of her back

SKYLIGHTS

(EH on his 1926 watercolor)

I do see the world triangularly
and there have often been times
that finely tight shape
moved past me to my paint,
as it did with this roofscape,
the building I had my studio in

The crunch of the scene attracted me:
the mortar smears on brick façades,
the vent pipe thrusts
and steep roofslopes,
and the narrow passageways
groined between them,

and an overcast sky that's limitless –
wedge after wedge of planes,
and abandonments of light
the hopeful call shadows –
but I call self

EVENING WIND

(EH on his 1921 etching)

The wind came up, she told me,
the moment she touched the bed
I hadn't even lain down, she said,
when a gust blew coolly in
and the curtain behind me swelled

For a moment, she said, I took it
as the ghost of a lost embrace,
perhaps a friend's sad last one,
though I haven't a notion who –
there haven't been that many,
she said, turning to look away

I remember, though, between
the last sketch and the etching,
something said, Tighten her up
as she glances out the window

I'm still not sure what it was
from the street that distracted her –
a cry, a brake scream, a wreck,
backfire or shot or shout –
maybe a memory turned her,
some past hope or fear recalled –
I don't know – I do know, though,
she did notice something
and I saw its effect, the way
it startled her – she was naked,
one knee up, kneeling on a bed

NEW YORK PAVEMENTS

(EH on his 1924–1925 oil)

God might well live in stone,
and I'm funnier, the riddler said,
than many think, and to show
the truth of this city that's home
I conjured a rushing nun
pushing a baby carriage
up a wind-blown empty street,

but the way the heavy blocks
of masonry and windowshades
receive the golden morning light
tells me again: someday yet
this city might truly turn gold

The templelike ionic columns,
the forward thrust of the porch,
the hurrying nun with her baby,
the golden glow transforming stone
and windowshade – all say

this strange place is holy

ELEVEN A.M.

(EH on his 1926 oil)

Geometry gives me the order I crave,
and today I've found it before noon
in a woman who's sitting naked,
triangular on a worn stuffed chair,
in a room whose window's wide open
to the eyes of the city and the wind

I don't know what she's looking at
I do know, though, it's not at grief,
and the mystery of her intensity
compells me to watch the way she sits
her chair, the way her interest in the street
allows the outside world to enter her,
her breasts and lap receptive,
but not, right now, to you or me

The fact she's kept her slippers on
underscores the ambiguity
of what this scene's about – it's not,
of course, an intimation of sin,
but it's also not a celebration
of spasms of loss or gain

The way she sits suggests an otherness:
sideways to me and her hair a mask,
and the way her form welcomes light
makes the slope of her back a line,

a syzygial line for morning light
to slide down, and the windowsill
suggests another line that moves
along the plane of her underthighs

But there's no discernible look in her eye:
she herself is triangularity,
and ghostlike echoes of that shape
spread throughout the room:
the patch of light in the picture frame
above the chest-of-drawers,
and at her feet the carpet's shape,
and the shape of the base of the lamp

HOTEL ROOM

(EH on his 1931 oil)

I know, in effect, who she is
but I don't know why
I keep seeing her there,
in a room that's better
than she can afford,
though I'm the one who placed her there,
and she won't be staying there,
she's much more transient than she knows,
sitting on the bed in her underwear,
a sheet of paper in her hands
and a shadow on her face
that's sheer but a mask –
and the sheet's three creases show
the paper's no letter
but a schedule for trains,
though I will have to add
the two, in effect, are the same

She's come to the city for work
and the boy back home has promised
he will do well in his job,
both for her and what he calls the plant,
and she finds the sentiment sweet
but no longer to the point
of what she is, and she doesn't know why,

though she is beginning to think
she won't go back
in the way she'd assumed she would,
and the fact she's reading the schedule
on the bed in her underwear
and imagining it's a letter
in a room dedicated to planes,
bags slovenly set near her feet
and her dress draped over the chair,
says she'll be friendly in time
with nakedness, though not
with the boy back home,
or anyone else she currently knows

Beds are containers for bedlam –
rectangular things often are –
like paintings, screens for screams,
motionless views of you and me –
perhaps that girl's a part of me,
a malleable part of me
and I'm the one who's reading the sheet
set on her knees:
                    the data no longer apply
but the sheet I'm reading allows me to flee

THE CITY

(EH on his 1927 oil)

I like the fact the city dwarfs us,
I like its expanses of breadth and height
and its wonderfully variant light
that can paint floor after floor
of a brick building's side
while holding twilight's haze intact

I like its monumental stillness,
its acceptance of asymmetry,
and though each building has its logic,
there's no inclusive plan of thrust
or slant or shape of window-way,
and the shadow-bruised skyline sprawls

on an overcast day when the grass
in the park is simply a plane,
like wall and street and time,
and only a few of us are out
The others were not welcome here
This is a painting I did of myself

MY ROOF

(EH on his 1928 watercolor)

As much as they seem like throughways
windows are planes to organize paint

Reds in the framelines and reds in brick,
reds on wood and the painted tin roof

are vibrant enough to be fictions here,
and they are, like windows, placed for form

Valuing my penchant to change
facts in my structureless world,

I also value the right to report
the arrogance of their homeliness

the way I've done here
with my building's cluttered roofline

whose hard nakedness seems sweet

ROOM IN BROOKLYN

(EH on his 1932 oil)

The light, passing by a vase,
seems to stop at her feet
but she's not the focal point
This is room and cityscape,
inside scene and outside scene,

and the room's the way I like it,
spacious and tastefully spare,
and if there are people about
outside, I can't see them there

No one mars my city's line,
and the woman with back to me
is a shadow-dimmed form,
not a voice interrupting me

NEW YORK MOVIE

(EH on his 1939 oil)

Backed pensively against the wainscoting
and a wall three lights have turned orange,
she wishes she believed she looked elegant
in this gabardine pantsuit they gave her
to usher the quality in – for she thinks
she should be among those on the screen,
and perhaps sometime I will be, she thinks,
wishing despair were an art, simply a pose
she knew how to affect, and she wonders,
as she stands, Will I ever let myself go,
let myself get lost from myself, and will
I ever stay anywhere long enough, or want
to stay in a place long enough to be able
to forget this grating desire I have
to flee this transient time of my life
and this room whose nostalgia-thick decor
apes a world none of us has lived in
People who stop here are transient, like me
They're on their way to or on their way from
less vibrant distractions, office or home –
little to crow about now in either place

If I could lose myself on the screen,
she thinks, I'd no longer want to run
upstairs, no longer want to flee this place –

I'd be where I want – then catching herself,
she stops, realizing she's been nicely lost
for a time, and chastened by that fact,
she asks herself – who else would I ask? –
if that upward path to her right goes out,
or ends upstairs in the loges that now
only lovers want – for the world's become
such a styleless, vulgar, diminished affair

But if, since I am not on the screen,
she thinks: if I ran, no one would notice
I had gone – the show's already begun
and there's nothing for me to do but wait
for the next succession of dreams
and dreamers who, like me, might fancy
they, too, could lose themselves,
they, too, could find a world they liked
in the chiaroscuro of the screen

OFFICE AT NIGHT

(EH on his 1940 oil)

I'm not that man
working at the desk –
he's a guy I invented,
and the woman turning toward him
is not ogling him,
she's simply someone
who'd like to skinny out
of her clinging clothes,
and the man, though he looks
like me except for his hair,
has lost himself in an invoice

The shade swells
at the woman's glance,
as if the guy subliminally knows –
no, she's the one who knows –
the power of flesh
cannot be contained
by file or desk or chain

NIGHTHAWKS

(EH on his 1942 oil)

They are not human, except in disguise
A hatchet-faced crew, their eyes
are sockets of darkness that catch no light

Forward-curving, their backs make them seem
as if they're perching on limbs
in a windless world where light, spilling out

from their aerie, triangulates all
the planes it touches: sidewalks
and streets, open windows, and wedge-lit walls

CITY SUNLIGHT

(EH on his 1954 oil)

The city reminds us how transient we are,
how briefly light lights on us,
lights singularly on us,
the light a clock whose ticks
record earth's constant shifts
the way a slipclad woman does
staring out a window
at the light that defines her

Objects that receive light paint light
as much as light paints them,
and dressed the way she is,
slipclad but ready to leave,
the woman says
she lives between antinomies,
but so do we

Changing colors, light changes shapes:
here a face and arms and breasts,
and there two tabletops
whose business mainly is
to serve as trays for planes of light

HOTEL WINDOW

(EH on his 1955 oil)

She's old but hard and fit
and though stuck on a sofa going nowhere
she looks like someone in passage,

and the unfluted column behind her
is a ghost from a past
that's not her past,
and the lay of the room
where she sits
suggests a power I don't understand

I know her mouth
I know her eyes and nose
I know the fullness of her breasts
and the firmness of her legs,

and I also know
that whoever she is
is a fiction,
an invention I need:
a hard, passing glance
that's mine, reflexively mine

SUNLIGHT IN A CAFETERIA

(EH on his 1958 oil)

I can draw figures
and light on walls
but not always the face
whose facile gestures
sometimes bother me

More to the point
is the fact I've cut
urban bustle out,
and the two I've left
are sitting alone
in a large room
where a vast flood of light
overwhelms the place,

the way one in France
who read me Verlaine
once overwhelmed me

Her face ceramic
as if it's a mask,
the young woman reads
her fingers and palms
while the youth
pretends to study
the brown flaring leaves
of the window plant

This dream keeps returning:
she's everywhere:
the blue of her dress
is in the chairs,
in the flowerpot's rim
and across the street
on the bottom step

Painting them, I paint
us all – I paint us
into symmetry,
the speech I know:

light a transient thing
entering this room,
overwhelming this room,

the way one in France
who read me Verlaine
once overwhelmed me

NIGHT WINDOWS

(EH on his 1928 oil)

Whether I'm dreaming, as I am now,
about her or the room she's in,
or aping lucidity as most of us do,
stairstep blocks of light
lead me toward her,
and like a gasp, the gauzelike curtain swells,
its pleats a sham of limbs
too removed, like her, for me to touch

And though I neither lament that
nor like that, I feel no guilt
about the fact that, back to me,
she's blind to me

But if you think I'm seizing her,
ramming her in my mind,
taking her against her will,
conjuring her into nothing more
than a lump I'd like to hump –
fine, think what you want –
but if you care about accuracy,
as so few do, consider the fact
she could just as well be my wife
as a stranger I've caught in a slip –

and considering that, consider that she
and the situation I've set her in

might be a fiction that helps me convey
that breath and flesh and desire
are tension-stirred rhythms of light,
and her building's ledge, so pubicly triangular,
is a world of stone
not so distant, damn you, from our own

"Night on the El Train" (1918)

British Museum of Art, London

NIGHT ON THE EL TRAIN

(EH on his 1918 etching)

What finally depressed them,
both of them literate,
was how clichéd their passion was:

the meeting in secret,
the banal vocabulary lovers use,
their unwillingness to junk

inconvenient mates –
I watched them and I saw
how when doubts crept in

they'd try to worry doubt away
Leaning together they'd try to believe
they were more than clichés

TRAIN & BATHERS

(EH on his 1920 etching)

You're likely inclined to say
I've counterpoised machine and life,
a locomotive crossing a bridge
and two nubile nudes
glancing at the train from the stream
they've been bathing in

The two are not equal, though
The train leans toward the girls,
machinery in debt, like me,
to the fact of flesh, neurally

But if you live within interstices –
and don't we all? In our day
ambiguity is synonym for home –
you learn to sing around tunes you hear,
you learn, also learn, sometimes learn
silence is better than the usual bawl
that comes when you assume your ecstasy
is something other than affliction,
and you might also learn
music often resides in sight,

and an arch beneath a trestle can be
the delta between a woman's thighs,
my woman's thighs, all thighs are hers
to me, and the texture of foliage seems

able to evoke the texture of hair
A part of the loud train's force,
I angle my attention toward
the naked presence of absentness

HOUSE BY THE RAILROAD

(EH on his 1925 oil)

I don't care now
that they tore it down
I do care though
there's no space left
where it was

The presence of space
surrounding verticality
intrigued me, as did
the fact that in memory
the walls assumed
the same cloudwash
that blurred the overcast sky

Now a strip mall crowds
the air where the house
stood oddly gabled
There's no space left
where space once was,

and the past is a dream I had

LOCOMOTIVE, D. & R.G.

(EH on his 1925 watercolor)

Santa Fe was too damn pretty,
Jo and I stuck all summer there,
and though the dry nights were cool
your nose bled all to hell,
and I didn't like the stuff
the natives had for sale –
turquoise and silver and corn beads –
though I did like the way the indios
seemed inclined to be distant,
sweetly laconic, like stone

That world, though, wasn't my world –
New Mexico a damn fool dream –
and for awhile I thought I'd go mad
in the idiotically thin air –
I didn't give a damn
about piñon pine and aspen stands
or a bunch of goddamn mountains
reputed to hemorrhage like the Lord

So one morning I split
I hadn't meant to frighten Jo
but she said she panicked
when waking up she found me gone,
for hours gone, scared all to hell
I'd gotten lost or gone nuts
on a whim of a morning's walk

I knew where the hell I was,
down in the railroad yard, at home
with my box of paints, a sheet
of good paper, and a big machine:
a steel-mawed engine whose puffs
outdid the anvil-topped thunderheads
Noise and oil and rust and track
worth a helluva lot more to me
than nature and pueblo crap
That's why when I did this piece
I left the goddamn background out

FREIGHT CARS, GLOUCESTER

(EH on his 1928 oil)

Drifting up out of despair
I spread a rust-red sweep
across the sides of railroad cars
and let the redness leap
onto chimneys and roofs
and higher still to the spires
on a distant steeple's base

The railroad cars had hauled me out
of a pit, my self-sized abyss,
and the secularly metal mass
blest me, and still blesses me
more than the gothic signs of God

Windblown weeds by the tracks
fanning into sunfire,
colors and shapes were offering me
the symmetry I need,
and even if I had to invent the effect –
dark pole braced by light-washed pole –
the triangle they made in my foreground
organized the mess I'd fallen in

SHOSHONE CLIFFS

(EH on his 1941 watercolor)

It took me awhile to accept the West
Santa Fe was too lyrically calm,
but this place had threats,
cliffs whose cleavages reminded me
what collision means:
glorious upheaval
and a splendid fall

HIGH NOON

(EH on his 1949 oil)

No trees to spoil the scenery,
the place itself has all I want:
a house for the light to strike
and a woman in the doorway
facing the sun with her robe undone

Indifferent to land and sky,
I like the way noon light,
slapping a white wall hard,
makes triangled shadow-fields
as sensual a presence as hair

CHURCH OF SAN ESTEBAN

(EH on his 1946 watercolor)

Colors in Saltillo sang sometimes
though afternoon rains messed up my light,
the dialect there was cricketlike
and the outdoor warm-meat market stank,
but the heat-struck short walls sang

Moorish in shape, St. Stephen's kept
a trinity of crosses in view on its dome,
white behind blue, squash-yellow with red,
and stuttered behind it, the fading echoes
of other religious structures rose:

a skeletally hollow belltower
and behind it a mosquelike dome
muttering the dun codes of earth,
the desert's scorched sand at home
slapping white glare onto walls,

and cloud-darkened, the mountains
nearby were fields of gray shadow,
and the sky went on forever
with no purpose whatever but to hold
the three cloud layers I invented

to make the pointless world right

EL PALACIO

(EH on his 1946 watercolor)

Five o'clock, cocktail time in Saltillo,
and the light has surrendered its glare
Tonight will likely be cool
but the clouds are wrong
for a long humming rain

This afternoon a shower passed
and stole my light, but the clouds
it left kept the glare away,
for awhile they kept the glare away,
and I'd rather not leave the window

The right light, I've found, is rare here,
so I'll do without the cocktail now,
and though there's a bustle of people about
down there where stores and movie are
the view from this angle is peopleless,

but the image, I'm sorry, won't last
except in the way I'm rendering it:
harmonies of light-washed rust
on mute cement and plaster walls,
and a stillness that's absolute

HOTEL BY A RAILROAD

(EH on his 1925 oil)

He's looking away from her, he's not
just gazing out the window,
and she's not looking at him, she's not
even looking at her book anymore
Why should she? How can she?
His interruptive silences assail her,

and they have, she thinks, for years,
and though the way he holds himself,
the way he always has, seems dignified,
he's erect in a desperate sort of way –
I know, for heavensakes, I know, she thinks,
I've failed his damn voluptuousness test,
and looking, I'm sure, slack and unslung,
I've drifted slumping into a slouch –
there's really no reason I shouldn't,
for mostly what we've done,
and have always done, is agitate ourselves
with ghosts we've never turned to friends,
and I'm sure we never will,
but it hurts to see him looking frail,
trying to be careful but just being stiff,
unable to do much more than stare
at the railroad tracks down there,
the ties rust-colored like the chest-of-drawers
and mirror frame in this room we're in

Does he think there's somewhere left
for him to go, other than deeper into despair,
that depressive place he took me years ago?
I know, I say, I've said it myself:
The world is named by planes
Colors and I do balancing acts
with blocks of color gesso shows through,
the lights and shadows as askew
as the stutter-limbed clowns
that dance their way through me
in ways the lady's always refused

CHAIR CAR

(EH on his 1965 oil)

They like us are transient things
contained by light,
and few connections match,
but the terror of facts like that
is even more meager
than expectations of delight

A brunette looks at a blonde
who looks at a book,
and a dark-hatted woman looks
at a man who looks
at the car's closed door –

almost everything points
at the car's closed door:
dusk-colored ceiling beams,
angles of window shades,
and the posture of the chairs

From the farthest window now
triangular light
segments the door,
but the door remains closed,

and light mats the floor
like four golden flags,

but the light will soon shift,
disappear for a time,
and glances will shift
and we'll all go blind

FOUR LANE ROAD

(EH on his 1956 oil)

In spite of a strong impulse toward tension
this is really a peaceful scene:
colors balanced and brushlines smooth,
as if we're sailing at high speed,
so except perhaps for the couple here
things seem geometrically clean,
though the woman's voice won't reach
her hatchet-faced husband's ear

Is that the source of his smile?
But she looks pleasant too,
though her forward lean says mean,
but she might be calling him pleasant things –
likely, though, she's not

Everything seems ambiguous here
Even the sweep of her chignonned hair
recalls a truncated auburn dream
I have never shaken loose from,
though the melony texture of her breasts
belongs, or belonged, to the woman
I've lived with for thirty-odd years,
very odd years, goddamn they've been odd

So who's being summoned here – the man
in the chair or me? And if me, who's calling me?

In both figures there's a troubling degree
of ambiguity I can't release,
but on the surface, the part I prefer,
calmness wins, which suggests,
at least to me, I've half-way understood
division's an acceptable thing

The blur of the road says time
is passing fast, the parts of the world
speeding by, as if mortality
is a weirdly rushed fact of life,
its parts always in counterflow,
and the world is a dream I've scarcely seen

WESTERN MOTEL

(EH on his 1957 oil)

Cezanne thought truth came in planes,
and Williams thought
ordinary matter's worth notice,
and both of them right, I live contained
by pigment and by mind,
with little use for God
who's never left a signature
on anything I've ever seen

I do, though, have my angels:
interplays of color and shape:
orange and red here,
and in the lamp and car
and shadows on walls
and mountain range
are murmurs of green,
vast murmurs of green

What seems least present
at times is most present,
and what seems most present,
the tall haughty blonde,
sitting board-backed as if
she thinks she needs to go somewhere,
is a fathomless thing

Colors about her have parallels in
her hair and eyes and skin,
each one a locus point for other things:
forehead and road, sill and shin

CALIFORNIA HILLS

(EH on his 1957 watercolor)

One day I saw a giant
in the massive hillslopes
of the Pacific Palisades,
a giant asleep in the hills,
or could he have been dead?
Or was he the patron
of the church set near here
on a site you can't see,
one I won't let you see,
and a bothersome cold,
the oddly pale sky says,
is blowing toward us fast

and all the shapes here,
recorded or invented,
I arranged triangularly,
the way I often do,
often need to do,
for colors are fictions too
See how whiteness works
its way up limblike slopes
You'd think it's predicting
the New England snows
I'll soon be foundering in,

but the flag
of earth's raw nakedness
that crowns the scene
is a brown that limns
rolling crests that echo
a slanted slab of brown
atop a slab of red:
the edge of a studio,
another thing manmade,
a preventive reminder here,
a mnemonic that my world
forbids you to drift
to places where sweetness sits

I've stopped time here
and even combined times,
but the day that stopped here
was rich with density
Light caressed the earth
but the giant stayed asleep,
and caliperlike shadows
triangled the road,
and the darkness road met
was sudden: the path a gasp
leading us into the world,
leading inside another world –
there are many worlds here:
the land, in short, California's,
but I couldn't finish there,
so the sky became Cape Cod's,
and the sleeping giant
is a ghost of God

SUMMER EVENING

(EH on his 1947 oil)

The porch tonight belongs to them
and the light they're in fortifies them,
and young, they've learned to speak
with a comfort I don't have,
and only a few I know have had

No anger bleeds on them tonight,
and though there's tension in them
no demons made them wooden-limbed
the way my figures have sometimes been
Somehow I quickly got them right

Leaning back against the balustrade,
her body brave with sensual speech,
she seems to be comfortable with
the kiss of light down all her length

The young man, though, is trigger-tight,
as I would be if she were mine,
though no junebugs or other pests
slap wall or door or face this time

"Italian Quarter, Gloucester" (1912)

The Whitney Museum of American Art, New York, NY

ITALIAN QUARTER, GLOUCESTER

(EH on his 1912 oil)

Large blocks of granite led me there,
and always to the back part
of the neighborhood

The place had no secrets
I was privy to, but the steep pitch
of the roof on the tallest home

drew me in, and the framed planes
of the buildings held me, and the sky
looked as uncertain as fate

Like the loud rasping speech
whose music somehow named me,
structures crowded together there,

rock planes pointing me through
the back parts of the neighborhood

LES DEUX PIGEONS

(EH on his 1920 etching)

The waiter is pleased
and the two old men are pleased
and I'm pleased – hell, we're all pleased:
the callow young man's been swept up
by a goodlooking girl
who knows how to love
Who wouldn't be pleased
by the lad's stroke of luck?
But part of me's still pissed
by what I left years ago

I know now and I knew then
what I was giving up,
and it wasn't simply France,
but what France means to me
So I'm glad for the young man,
and glad I was once overwhelmed myself
by a woman who'd not been starched stiff
by the goddamn church

But hell on that
There's at least compensation,
coded as it is,
in that years ago
I was somehow smart enough
to make this etching laugh,
and detached enough
to let it laugh at me

THE LIGHTHOUSE

(EH on his 1923 etching)

Everything else is defined on all sides:
the homes, the boulder juts and rolls,
the waves washing back out to sea,

but the lighthouse dissolves into sky,
the rounded turns of a shadow's length
disappearing into the endless light

ST. FRANCIS' TOWERS

(EH on his 1925 watercolor)

Mencken, of course, would come to lament
America's libido for ugliness,
but the fact bothered him, not me:
a lot of us like grotesquerie,
and these towers rising steeplelessly,
as if the longing for God had been cut
by a church committee's vote,
appeal to me – their raw vitality
supplants as well as complements
their weirdly modest piety

No lights shine from the portholes,
and no ghost of a rose window's there,
and no stained glass enchants
worshiper or passerby, and the fence-
like walls near the street look make-
shift, like these last line-breaks,
and even though they're graffitiless
they seem, though unmessed, unkempt –
the area has drifted to seed

Carelessly moving toward decay,
America's had no time to get
spasmed up with grief, or be
nostalgic, except for the fiction of Eden,
that ridiculous pissant place,

and I accept and even affirm that,
and I'm doing so with my image here,
but it's wrong to label me
and my like-minded time-mates
as realistic raconteurs,
for we've defined modernity –
we haven't simply mimicked it –
and in our own odd kind of joy
in celebrating urbanity we've embraced
the darker threats, the shadow-worlds,
without euphemizing vulgarity

But before I let my rage out,
and believe me, it will come out,
I'll admit I'm as icy-hearted
as our circus of a world is ugly
Keeping my lyrical impulses at bay,
and inclined to help disaster strike,
I've signed these roofs with checks of light

DRUG STORE

(EH on his 1927 oil)

I know this looks like reportage
but it's fiction, an invention
of reds and blues and greenish blacks
in a grid whose gestures
chant mysteries to me –
triangularities everywhere,
from the shadows on sidewalks
to the lanterns of lamps,
and bunting furled in the window display

Triangularities are everywhere,
but irregularities are common, too,
and the building's roofline slopes,
for awhile it seems to slope,
a trick of my painting's topmost edge,
another illusion to alter scope

And brash, the window sign's no stoppage
but an opening, a passage to a back wall,
but the wall pushes back
through the letters of the sign:
an interplay of tensions there,
as if night itself does not mean absentness,
though it does: everything that seems organic
comes from a symmetry I impose
There is no God, and tonight
light is manmade, and elixirs

are scarcely effectual things,
pagan vitality impossible now,
and the drug store is earth and church:
the boxes of bandages there: signs
of the presence of the absence
of God, and in that fact I find
neither source of fear nor source of pride,
but a gesture of comfort: I like the fact
no walkers are out to mar my night

EAST WIND OVER WEEHAWKEN

(EH on his 1934 oil)

Only the grass, the uncut dead grass,
shows where the wind is,
shows how neglect has marked the yards,

and the day, like the year,
severely overcast and late,
is cold and damp,

but only the grass, the uncut dead grass,
shows where the wind is,
and it points away from the men,

the darkly wrapped small men
who are as anonymous here
as they'll be when dead,

a cluster of unconnected men
near my painting's far left edge

But only the grass, the uncut dead grass,
says where the wind is,
and none of the windows I've done

reflects a glance of errant light,
and the two utility poles lean
aslant near the corner's street lamp,
but only the grass, the uncut dead grass,
shows where the wind is

CAPE COD EVENING

(EH on his 1939 oil)

Hell yes she's unhappy:
alone out here near the woods
with her troglodytic mate
spending too much time
tossing trinkets for a dog,

and dressed up, too,
she's hot to go somewhere,
but she knows they won't:
they'll stay talkless here,
there's little to say,

and too many battles
battle within them
for them to believe again
golden waves of grass
or forests of dancing firs

have anything to offer them

THE LEE SHORE

(EH on his 1941 oil)

Clouds, like the sails, have caught the wind
that tosses the waves that pitch the boats,
and though shelter's near
I'll strain away
from the roundness of the porch
that's treacherous with its own kind of will

Even the grass on the shore leans seaward,
away from the refuge of land,
but the long lawn cuts
the slant of the waves triangularly,
and even the sweep of the grass
projects a ghost in the sky

Like gestures of hope, the prows of two boats
point toward a third in the sea,
and though the current brings us shoreward,
geometry and will take us seaward once more

SEVEN A.M.

(EH on his 1948 oil)

The darkness is there
just beyond the light
and, like death, it's quick,

as sharp a point of interest now
as the comforting symmetry
of the shop's front window,

the art-stopped clock telling time
while a wind, fanning the trees,
sweeps the boughs into a blur

The darkness there in the firs:
a balance for geometry,
the certainty of straight lines,

a certainty so complete
I simply don't care
if the lines stand or slant

The world, like the morning,
is in transit, and no one
is present to bother that fact

FOUR DEAD TREES

(EH on his 1942 watercolor)

1

There seem to be two paths,
light and sky, darkness and earth

The wheelruts, though, curve right,
sliding through sand-colored grass
to a wooded valley –
that's the main path,
an entrance into dense shadow

But out of darkness
another darkness rises:
long thin layers of clouds
pulling us skyward
into a planar wedge of blue

2

Barkless and ashenly white,
the shortest tree, the one that's straight,
is a gateless gate post
that centers everything

Three trees, though, remain –
two with arms, one with head

They reach toward the sky,
a cool triangular blue
moving into white

Like devotees in ecstasy,
they sing us away from Earth

toward another world
I've never been able to see

SUMMERTIME

(EH on his 1943 oil)

It's good you noticed, if you did
A number, I'll say, have not come close
This one's a nude, the clothes a guise,
a mask, a witty, illusory stab
at idiot propriety – imagination strips
everything bare, as I've done here:
the nipples and heft of breasts in view
and the screaming delight of thighs
rising toward the truth between them,
as suggested by the curtain's cleft –
all this a celebration of my mood,
and my mood trumps anything that's yours

This lass, who looks sweetly nubile now,
is Jo, my wife, whose age has been reduced
by the cleverness of my brush and paint
I've stripped her nearly bare, but I
have also preserved defiant ghosts
in the willful set of her swelling lips

The tensions and songs here are mine
You can do with your own what you will

OFFICE IN A SMALL CITY

(EH on his 1953 oil)

The issue is not
what the man is staring at,
the issue is
the despair I feel
when in my rage
I will not name
the slight or ghost
that's offended me

Perhaps my walls are thick,
but the windows here,
as mine tend to be, are glassless,
and alien to speech
they're alien to rage

As I've envisioned things,
the man at his desk,
his eyes downcast
but his posture fine,
seems to write or draw
on an unfurled sheet of light,
the only flag I know

My windowpanes are planes of air,
and all of interest on the desks
are oblong slabs of light
that turn the dark wood gold
and turn the concrete white

ROOMS BY THE SEA

(EH on his 1951 oil)

I, too, like Magritte
but our points of weirdness
aren't the same

Light on the wall
and the sea out the door
are sufficient for me

I don't need people
floating goofball through my skies
or breasting through my walls

Inanimate things,
like planes of light, door and sea,
speak well enough for me

Nothing's inviting me out
into oblivion of sky or sea,
and nothing says stay put

Nothing, in fact, addresses me

SEA WATCHERS

(EH on his 1952 oil)

See the way he leans, forward sprung,
as if he hopes the sea might take him,
but it won't, he knows it won't

Now see the way she sits, poised,
but the tuck of her chin shows
she's withholding what she knows

Even when bitter she'll stay controlled
Either she can't or won't explode

He leans forward, she leans back,
their doubles the pylons on the left,
bound by chains with rusted links,

and the wind that whips these two
whips the swipes of white in the sky,
the overcast sky of an angry brush
measuring the weather in these two

while oddly rippleless, the sea speaks
with a vast, flat placidity
I confess I wish I knew

CAROLINA MORNING

(EH on his 1955 oil)

I never found out
if she really was a hooker:
I don't and didn't care

I liked the abruptness
of her sullenness,
her hard but voluptuous lips,

and her hands as hidden as her heart

The shutters of her place
were in need of repair,
but the field off her porch was a sea

My god she had sass!
Look at the way she stands:
leaning backward to avoid us

but her left leg forward:
you'd think she's Egyptian,
a goddess or consort on leave,

someone whose rearing,
whose meetings with grief
have made her indifferent
to the fact that time,
disappearing in the sky,
disappears in the sea

MASS OF TREES AT EASTHAM

(EH on his 1962 watercolor)

There's nothing, goddamnit, wrong
with my eyes and it's not that here,
near what seems the end,
I'm turning abstract
in a way I've not been

The world, as I know it, is fields of light,
and it's only there that I find voice –
there are no ideas outside light –
and what I've done here
is what I've always done:
chuck anything that's crap

I like these trees, I like the depth
of their greenness, the effect
of the yellowness of the river
cutting widely between the vast stands,
between the trees and where I am

River and bank as one suits me fine,
and I like the hardness
of the streaks in the clouds,
I like the notion
that spreads of light in the trees
seem like flashes, early flashes
of a huge conflagratory fire:
sand and water becoming flame

But not too far from here
the distant bend in the river
follows a shadow's arrow point
to a place I can't see
and have not seen
and will never, I'm sorry, see
I'm blinded by masses
of light and trees

SUN IN AN EMPTY ROOM

(EH on his 1963 oil)

No, hell no, I was not
meditating on death
or notions of emptiness
I meant what I presented:
unadorned slabs of light
on two unaddled walls,

but when you asked
what I was looking for
in peopleless planes,
I said, *Myself – what else?*
for light is where self is
if self itself ever is

Neither misery nor peace
finds voice or home here,
though a window does
and with it a blur of leaves,
salves for a claustrophobe
There's nothing abstract here,

and nothing metaphorical,
and except for several ghosts
of gridmarks I've left
all planes are walls or floor,
and chiaroscuro is flesh,
and shadows, stains to mark
where light finds speech

TWO COMEDIANS

(EH on his 1966 oil)

Perhaps it's the costume
that lets me laugh,
or smile as it were –
for me they've been the same

Perhaps it's the clown's disguise
that lets me be
looser than I usually am
strutting cock-proud now,
goofy-eyed at a crowd,
the illusion of a crowd
no one sees but you and me

Clowns, we move toward stage's edge,
a place I've made like a roof's edge,
with threat or promise of a fall

But the moment seems sweet,
our domestic wars almost done,
and white-clad and foolscapped,
we seem blest as we press
toward the last edge we'll meet,

our lyrical selves always in France,
our final days just bibelots:
Nous sommes, Jo et moi, les pierrots

INDEX OF PAINTINGS AND ETCHINGS
BY EDWARD HOPPER

ABOUT THE AUTHOR

James Hoggard's work in multiple genres has routinely been called "brilliant." A poet, short story writer, novelist, playwright, essayist and translator, he is the author of nineteen books and recipient of numerous awards, including, in 2006, the Lon Tinkle Award for Excellence Sustained Throughout a Career. He has also been Poet Laureate of Texas and a two-term president of the Texas Institute of Letters.

His novel *Trotter Ross* (Wings, 1999) was called "far and away the finest novel about masculine coming of age in current American literature" by Leonard Randolph, former director of the National Endowment for the Arts Literature Program. Writing about *Patterns of Illusion: Short Stories & A Novella*, the novelist John Nichols said, "Hoggard knows as much as anyone on earth about the small tender mercies and brutalities of people ... a truly wonderful writer." His most recent collection of poems, *Wearing The River* (Wings, 2005), received the PEN Southwest Poetry Award.

In addition to appearing in periodicals such as *Harvard Review, Southwest Review, Words Without Borders, Manoa, Tri-Quarterly, Arts & Letters, Image, Massachusetts Review, Partisan Review,* and many other journals and anthologies, his work has also appeared in India, England, Canada, and the Czech Republic. He's given readings and lectures at universities throughout the U.S. as well as in Mexico, Cuba, and Iraq. A noted literary translator, Hoggard was chosen to give the University Professors Lecture On Literary Translation and Theory at Boston University.

Hoggard is the Perkins-Prothro Distinguished Professor of English at Midwestern State University in Wichita Falls, Texas.

Wings Press was founded in 1975 by Joanie Whitebird and Joseph F. Lomax, both deceased, as "an informal association of artists and cultural mythologists dedicated to the preservation of the literature of the nation of Texas." Publisher, editor and designer since 1995, Bryce Milligan is honored to carry on and expand that mission to include the finest in American writing—meaning all of the Americas, without commercial considerations clouding the choice to publish or not to publish.

Wings Press attempts to produce multicultural books, chapbooks, CDs, DVDs and broadsides that, we hope, enlighten the human spirit and enliven the mind. Everyone ever associated with Wings has been or is a writer, and we know well that writing is a transformational art form capable of changing the world, primarily by allowing us to glimpse something of each other's souls. Good writing is innovative, insightful, and interesting. But most of all it is honest.

Likewise, Wings Press is committed to treating the planet itself as a partner. Thus the press uses as much recycled material as possible, from the paper on which the books are printed to the boxes in which they are shipped.

As Robert Dana wrote in *Against the Grain*, "Small press publishing is personal publishing. In essence, it's a matter of personal vision, personal taste and courage, and personal friendships." Welcome to our world.

WINGS PRESS

Colophon

This first edition of *Triangles of Light: The Edward Hopper Poems*, by James Hoggard, has been printed on 70 pound paper containing fifty percent recycled fiber. Titles have been set in Herculanum type, the text is in Adobe Caslon type. All Wings Press books are designed and produced by Bryce Milligan.

On-line catalogue and ordering:
www.wingspress.com

Wings Press titles are distributed
to the trade by the
Independent Publishers Group
www.ipgbook.com
and in Europe by
www.gazellebookservices.co.uk